Animals in Danger

in Australia

Louise and Richard Spilsbury

Raintree is an imprint of Capstone Global Library Limited, a company incorporated in England and Wales having its registered office at 7 Pilgrim Street, London, EC4V 6LB – Registered company number: 6695582

www.raintreepublishers.co.uk
myorders@raintreepublishers.co.uk

Text © Capstone Global Library Limited 2013
First published in hardback in 2013
Paperback edition first published in 2014
The moral rights of the proprietor have been asserted.

Edited by Rebecca Rissman, Dan Nunn, and Adrian Vigliano
Designed by Philippa Jenkins
Picture research by Tracy Cummins
Originated by Capstone Global Library Ltd
Printed in China by South China Printing Company Ltd

ISBN 978 1 406 26207 0 (hardback)
17 16 15 14 13
10 9 8 7 6 5 4 3 2 1

ISBN 978 1 406 26214 8 (paperback)
18 17 16 15 14
10 9 8 7 6 5 4 3 2 1

British Library Cataloguing in Publication Data
A full catalogue record for this book is available from the British Library.

Acknowledgements
We would like to thank the following for permission to reproduce photographs: Alamy pp. 9 (© Ken Hobson), 18 (© Ethan Daniels); FLPA pp. 22 (Martin B Withers), 26 (Eric Woods); Getty Images pp. 6 (Visuals Unlimited, Inc./Dave Watts), 11 (Ted Mead); Gunther Schmida p. 23 (© Gunther Schmida); istockphoto pp. 21 (© Craig Dingle), 29 (© Joe Potato Photo); Nature Picture Library p. 17 (© Brent Hedges); NHPA p. 15 (A.N.T. PHOTO LIBRARY); Shutterstock pp. 4 (© Chris P.), 5 bottom (© Andres Ello), 5 top (© edella), 28 (© KWL), icons (© Florian Augustin), (© tristan tan), maps (© AridOcean); Superstock pp. 10, 13, 14 (© Minden Pictures), 19 (© Science Faction), 25 (© NHPA), 27 (© Gerard Lacz Images).

Cover photograph of a southern cassowary reproduced with permission of SuperStock (© Minden Pictures). Cover photograph of red tailed black cockatoos reproduced with permission of Shutterstock (© John Carnemolla). Cover photograph of orange stones reproduced with permission of Shutterstock (© Martin Horsky). Cover photograph of Green Sea Turtle reproduced with permission of istockphoto (© sweetlifephotos). Cover photograph of a numbat reproduced with permission of istockphoto (© Craig Dingle).

We would like to thank Michael Bright for his invaluable help in the preparation of this book.

Every effort has been made to contact copyright holders of any material reproduced in this book. Any omissions will be rectified in subsequent printings if notice is given to the publisher.

[...] ...book were
[...] ...ue to the
[...] ...s may
[...] ...eased to
[...] ...ublisher
[...] ...rs, no
[...] ...epted by

Contents

Where is Australia?......................... 4

Animals of Australia...................... 6

Western Australia 8

Northern Territory 12

Queensland 16

Southeastern Australia 20

South Australia 25

Helping Australia's animals 28

Glossary...................................... 30

Find out more............................... 32

Index 32

Some words are shown in bold, **like this.** You can find out what they mean by looking in the glossary.

Where is Australia?

We divide the world into seven large areas of land called **continents**. Australia is the smallest continent in the world. It is mostly hot and dry in Australia, but there are different places for animals to live.

NORTH AMERICA

EUROPE

ASIA

ATLANTIC OCEAN

AFRICA

PACIFIC OCEAN

PACIFIC OCEAN

SOUTH AMERICA

INDIAN OCEAN

AUSTRALIA

N
W   E
S

ANTARCTICA

Can you see the continent of Australia?

scrubland

What type of habitats can you see in Australia?

The **habitats** in Australia range from thick woodlands, to **scrubland**, **deserts**, and rivers. As an island, Australia is also surrounded by sea.

Animals of Australia

Some animals in Australia are **endangered.** This means there are very few of that type of animal left. If they all die, that type of animal will be **extinct.** Animals that are extinct are gone from the planet forever.

Sadly, the bridled nailtail wallaby of Australia is endangered.

Different types of animals look and behave differently from each other. We sort them into groups to help tell them apart.

Animal classification chart

Amphibian	• lives on land and in water • has damp, smooth skin • has **webbed** feet • lays many eggs	
Bird	• has feathers and wings • hatches out of hard-shelled eggs	
Fish	• lives in water • has **fins** and most have **scales** • young hatch from soft eggs	
Mammal	• drinks milk when a baby • has hair on its body	
Reptile	• has scales on its body • lives on land • young hatch from soft-shelled eggs	

Look out for pictures like these next to each photo. They will tell you what type of animal each photo shows.

Western Australia

Some animals in Western Australia are **endangered** because their woodland **habitats** are being destroyed. People cut trees to sell the wood, to build towns, or to make fields to grow **crops** on.

This is a map of Western Australia.

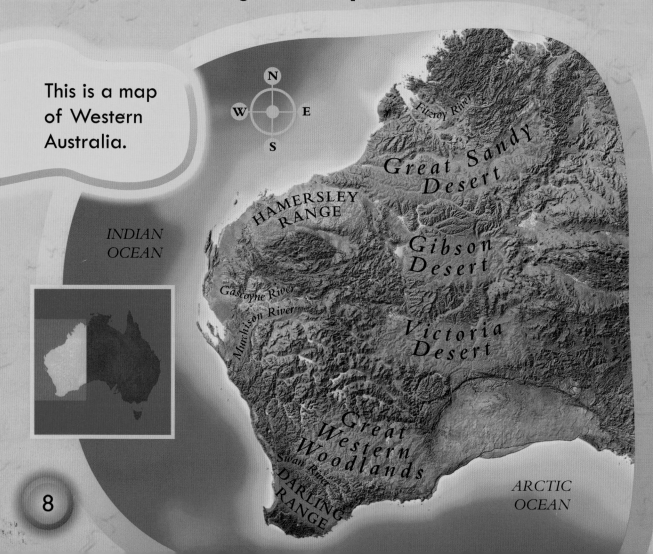

The red-tailed black cockatoo makes its nest high up in tree trunks. With fewer trees, it has less food and fewer places to make nests.

This cockatoo uses its huge beak to crack open seeds from trees to eat.

The numbat sleeps on branches or in hollow logs at night. By day, it hunts for **insects** called termites. Its strong claws dig up termite nests. It uses its long, sticky tongue and small, sharp teeth to catch termites.

The numbat is the size of a squirrel.

The red-tailed phascogale has grooved pads on its feet to help it climb trees.

During the day, the red-tailed phascogale rests in tree holes lined with leaves. It eats insects and other small animals at night. It finds most food on the ground, but jumps high in the air to catch birds, too!

Northern Territory

Some **endangered** animals in the Northern Territory live in **scrubland** or **deserts**. It is very hot and rarely rains here. Dry plants catch fire easily, and fires spread quickly. Farm animals eat many plants, too.

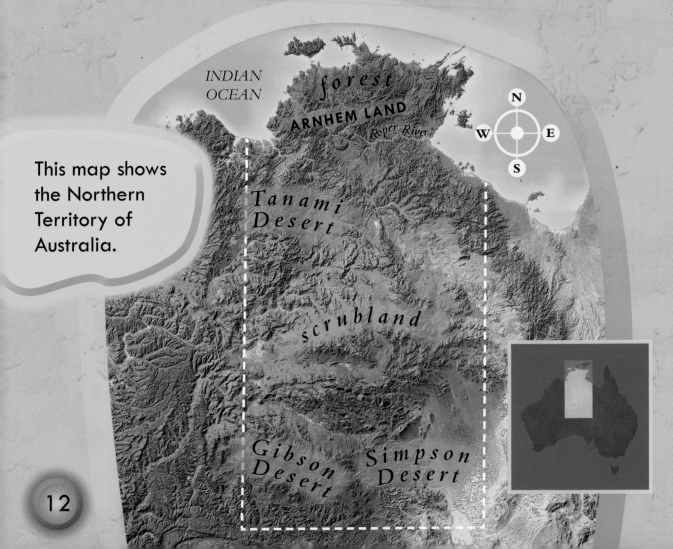

This map shows the Northern Territory of Australia.

INDIAN OCEAN

forest

ARNHEM LAND

Roper River

N
W   E
S

Tanami Desert

scrubland

Gibson Desert

Simpson Desert

Great desert skinks work together to dig large, deep burrows. They hide from the scorching sun in burrows during the day. Fires can wipe out the plants and **insects** that the skinks come out to eat during the cooler evening.

Like many desert animals, skinks get most of the water they need from their food.

The western bilby's sharp claws rake insects out of the soil and dig deep burrows. The bilby rests in burrows during the day to avoid the heat and **predators** such as snakes. Fewer plants mean fewer insects for the bilby to eat.

A bilby uses its big ears to listen for predators and its long nose to sniff for food at night.

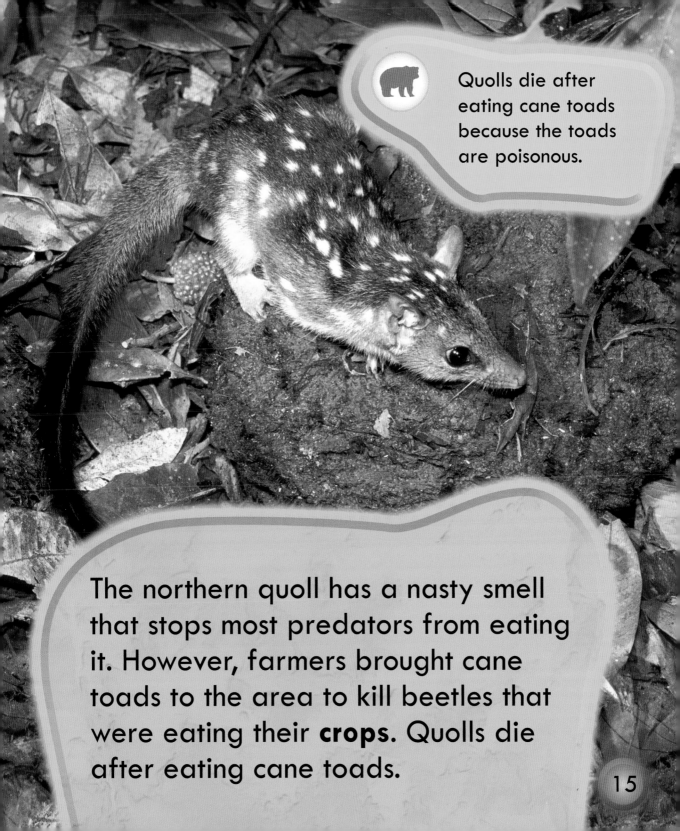

Quolls die after eating cane toads because the toads are poisonous.

The northern quoll has a nasty smell that stops most predators from eating it. However, farmers brought cane toads to the area to kill beetles that were eating their **crops**. Quolls die after eating cane toads.

15

Queensland

Some **endangered** animals in Queensland live in forests and in the ocean around the **Great Barrier Reef**. People cut down trees to build homes and farms. They trap some animals in fishing nets by mistake.

Can you see rivers on this map of Queensland?

Mitchell River

Flinders River

Woodland

Burdekin River

GREAT BARRIER REEF

GREAT DIVIDING RANGE

PACIFIC OCEAN

N
W E
S

The northern hairy-nosed wombat digs deep burrows with many tunnels. It rests during the day and comes out at night to eat plants. One reason it is endangered is that farm animals eat its plants.

This wombat got its name because it has so many whiskers!

17

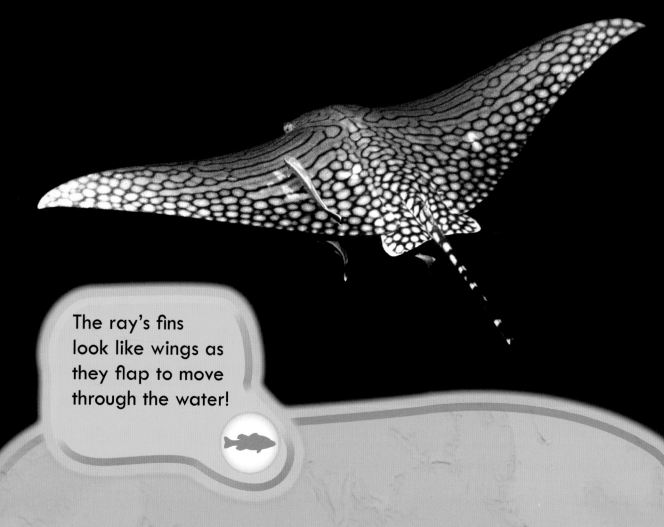

The ray's fins look like wings as they flap to move through the water!

Ornate eagle rays flap their huge **fins** to move through the water. They swim along the ocean floor looking for shellfish to crush with their flat teeth. Sadly, many rays are trapped in fishing nets and die.

Female green turtles come to beaches at night to dig nests with their back **flippers**. They lay 100 eggs and cover them with sand. Two months later, babies hatch out of the eggs and race to the sea!

Green turtles are endangered because people eat them and their eggs, and use their nesting beaches.

Southeastern Australia

Some animals in southeastern Australia are **endangered** because of **introduced** animals that people brought here. People bring new animals for food or to kill **pests**.

GREAT DIVIDING RANGE

Darling River

_ _ River

Murrumbidgee River

forests

PACIFIC OCEAN

▲ Mount Kosciuszko (2,229 metres)

This is southeastern Australia.

N
W   E
S

TASMANIA

People brought foxes to kill rabbits, but the foxes eat the Tasmanian devil's food, too.

The Tasmanian devil has powerful **jaws** and strong teeth for crushing animal bones. At night, it sniffs out dead animals to eat. It screeches loudly at other animals that try to take its food!

People put mosquito fish in rivers to catch and eat insects, but the fish eat lots of frog eggs as well.

Growling grass frogs can grow up to 10 centimetres (4 inches) long! They live among plants at the edges of streams and ponds. Males make growling sounds to attract females to lay eggs in the water.

Trout cod live in fast-flowing rivers and shelter under fallen branches. They eat **insects**, shrimp, and fish. Introduced rainbow trout compete with them for food, and introduced brown trout eat their young.

Trout cod can leap from the water to catch insects just above the surface.

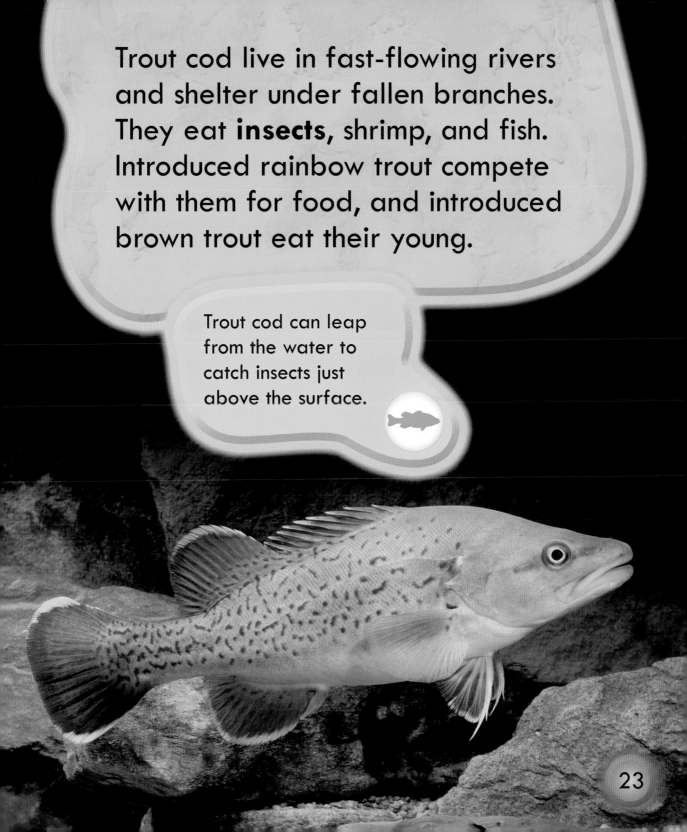

This agile possum can leap long distances from tree to tree.

The Leadbeater's possum needs forests to survive. It makes its nests in old, hollow trees. It eats **insects** and spiders from behind tree **bark**.

South Australia

Some **endangered** animals in South Australia live in forests and **scrublands**. People cut trees to sell the wood. They take over land for sheep and other farm animals to **graze** on and to grow **crops**.

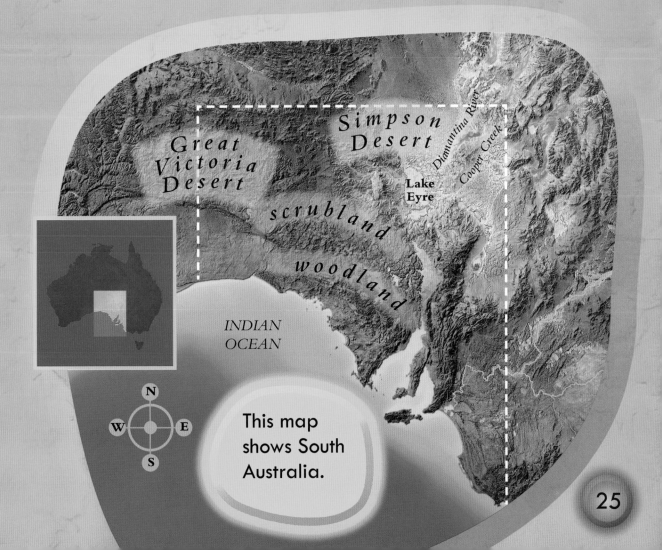

Great Victoria Desert

Simpson Desert

Diamantina River

Cooper Creek

Lake Eyre

scrubland

woodland

INDIAN OCEAN

N W E S

This map shows South Australia.

Malleefowl nests are huge holes in the ground filled with plants. The plants rot and make heat to keep this bird's eggs warm. When malleefowl chicks hatch, they dig their own way out of the mound.

Today, there is less space for malleefowl to make nests and fewer plants to eat.

The woylie hops through scrublands on its back legs.

The woylie's amazing tail can grasp and carry bundles of grass! The woylie needs lots of grass to make nests. It also sniffs out underground mushrooms to eat and digs them up with its sharp claws.

Helping Australia's animals

In Australia, there are **reserves** to protect animals. These are areas of land where animals live safely. There are also laws to stop people from hunting or hurting **endangered** animals.

People used to hunt koalas for their fur. Now, laws protect them from hunters.

Make sure any outdoor pets wear bells on their collars to prevent them from catching birds and other small animals.

We can all do little things to help wild animals.

Glossary

bark outer covering of a tree

continent one of seven large areas that make up the world's land

crop food plant

desert hot, dry area of land often covered with sand and few plants

endangered when a type of animal is in danger of dying out

extinct no longer alive; not seen in the wild for 50 years

fin flat body part that sticks out of a fish's body and helps it steer and move

flipper wide, flat arm that some animals use for swimming

graze to eat grass

Great Barrier Reef huge coral reef. A coral reef is a rocky structure formed by many tiny animals.

habitat place where plants and animals live

insect small animal with six legs, such as an ant or fly

introduced animal brought by people to a new area

jaws part of an animal's body that contains its mouth and often teeth

pest animal that eats a farmer's plants

predator animal that catches and eats other animals for food

reserve large area of land where plants and animals are protected

scale small, overlapping pieces that cover an animal's body

scrubland hot, dry area of land with many bushy plants and sandy soil

webbed when feet have skin between the toes

Find out more

Books

Australasia's Most Amazing Animals (Animal Top Tens), Anita Ganeri (Raintree, 2008)

Endangered Animals (Trailblazers), David Orme (Ransom Publishing, 2009)

Internet sites

gowild.wwf.org.uk

Go Wild is the children's club of WWF. You can learn about different animals and their habitats.

www.oum.ox.ac.uk/thezone/animals/extinct/index.htm

Find out about some animals that are now extinct on this website.

Index

amphibian 7
bird 7, 11, 26, 29
crop 8, 15, 25
desert 5, 8, 12, 13, 25
fish 7, 22, 23
graze 25

habitat 5, 8
mammal 7
pest 20
predator 14, 15
reptile 7
scrubland 5, 12, 25, 27